Dark Emotions

Mya Torres

BookLeaf Publishing

Presentation by *BookLeaf Publishing*

Web: www.bookleafpub.com

E-mail: info@bookleafpub.com

ISBN: 9789357213257

First edition 2023

Instead Of

Instead of dying,
I take to paper and pen.
To canvas and to acrylic,
And I pour this pain in which we call life
Until I have been drained of this terrible feeling
And I finally feel like I can live
Instead of dying.

What We Are

I have made love to his body and to his soul
Intertwined in both the astral plane
And on his bed.
His legs touching mine,
Two souls merging into one.
This is what we are.

Inner Peace Vs. Depression

I have been manic for so long
That the quiet in my head astounds me.
I am confused as to whether it's depression
Or if I’ve finally found inner peace.

Rotten Love

We were victims of our immaturity,
Victims of the obsession running unchecked in our hearts
The fiery flame of passion and lust sitting inside our teenaged frames.
No one taught us how to love properly,
Of how to react and how to forgive.
That is why we now bear the ugly scars
Of a rotten kind of love.

Liquid Courage

He didn't ask why I was crying as I sat across him
But had he asked
I would have said this,
"There have been many instances,
Those in which I assumed you didn't love me
But this moment in time assured me.
I don't have to assume anymore,
And I see it clearly despite my intoxicated state.
In fact, the liquid gave me the courage to pack up my bags
And leave
Before you rub yet more salt into my wounds.
You truly don't love me,
And this is okay."

Set Free

Writing sets me free because unlike people,
The pages do not judge me nor do they taunt me for what I feel.
They do not belittle me.
Instead,
Writing wraps its arms around me,
And I feel loved.

Empty

I wonder if some day I will stop feeling the
empty.
Feeling so cold and so bruised.
I don’t want to feel this way anymore.
I want to feel warm,
Like spring in midday.
Or perhaps an orange sunset.
Instead I am the embodiment of winter,
Carrying on its wish of death.

Moon

I look up to the skies only to find the pale moon
staring back at me.
I wonder if you are looking at the moon at this
very moment too.
Reminiscing the sweet nothings and gangly
embraces we once shared on a night like this.
I wonder if you even think of me at all.

All or Not At All

You love me all
Or you don’t love me at all
I am not an idea
Nor am I a theory
In which you can fascinate yourself with
Until you realize I am not what your mind made me out to be.
You love me all,
My flaws and my eccentricity
Everything that makes me who I am,
Or you don’t love me at all.

Extremes

I've lingered between too much and too little my entire life.
From not sleeping a wink,
To sleeping for 14 hours straight.
From intense feelings of numbness,
To crying at the slightest of things.
It's black or it's white,
Not a gray area in sight.
My life is built on extremes.
From negative to positive
Perhaps this is why I feel jaded.
Living life like this is exhausting.

Lungs

My lungs are full of water,
Akin to a newborn.
I am struggling to breathe,
But I can only suffocate.
I cannot adjust to a new environment,
And unlike a newborn,
I won't take that breath that will free me.
That breath between life and death.
I will die.

Puzzle

I am a puzzle that's been opened by a careless owner,
An owner that lost my pieces
And because I was no longer complete,
Threw me away.
Who will want me now when you've lost all the pieces that made me whole?

High

He made me feel something
That to this day
I still chase the high,
Despite finding it nowhere.
Not in the way I shoot neon in my veins.
Not even then do I feel
The immensity that I felt
As we laid side by side
And I stared into bright emerald eyes.

Mother's Daughter

I am my mother's daughter
A fool that stays with another out of longing
Even if I do not see the love anymore.
And like her,
I stay with the hopes
That I wake up one day to find that he truly loves me.
I am my mother's daughter.
In her suffering and her bad decisions.
In both her softness and her cruelty.
This is okay though.
I am my mother's daughter after all.

If He Had Never Met Me

I see old pictures of him and I recognize the
little boy.
I recognize the features and the youth.
But my mind cannot fathom.
It cannot fathom that the
Bitter and hopeless person he has become,
Could have possibly
At one point in his life,
been that happy boy on a sunny afternoon.
All the pain I have caused him.
The anger and the melancholia.
He cannot see a future anymore,
Not like he did before.
He is himself,
But not the version he could have been.
Therefore I have a reasoning in my mind.
A reasoning born Not out of spite but one of
regret.
It goes like this.
How happier he could have been,
If he had never met me.

Cigarette

I feel like a cigarette.
No matter how hard he tries to quit me,
He always come back for one more drag.
Im not good for his health and he knows this,
Yet he still comes back for one more, and one
more.
Only after years of inhaling my addictive toxins
does he realize that they are burrowed deep
inside his lungs.
My poisons have infected his body.
He feels as if he's suffocating
And sickness has ravaged his form.
Even ill he can't seem to put me down.
He should have set me down rather than put me
against his lips for so long.
I feel like a cigarette.
Deadly and addictive because his love for me
will slowly but surely kill him.

Cycle

All I needed was tenderness.
A gentle hand guiding me into light.
All I received was a harsh one,
Guiding me to be the cruel one I am.
The abuser molded me and the victim dissolved.
I grew to be the abuser.
And the cycle swallowed me into its loop.

Letters

Letters,
Those in which he wrote me
When we were in high school.
How I miss that child.
He is a strong man now.
I wonder where the years went.
Oh these beautiful letters,
His ode to me.
When he finally left,
These same letters that I once looked at with joy,
I then wept to.
I cried and I cried.
Staining them with a river of tears.

Father

My father is a good man in his old age.
I love him.
But he wasn't always good.
I am part my father.
Half of him built my existence,
Therefore this weathered face I wear is my fathers.
But I too wear his terrible anger,
This hot tempered blood in my veins is his.
The anger though,
It did not come from genes.
It came from a lack of tenderness.
A lack of not love, but understanding.
I needed a father when the world had me by the throat.
But I only had myself.

Blood

I think about the poetry I write
How beautiful it seems to leak onto the pages.
But then I think,
It was not beautiful then.
It was bloody and raw,
And so I took my hands and turned it into
beautiful poetry
Adding meaning to the pain I've felt.
Something much more than just blood spilt.
That way, it will have been worth it,
To lose a liquid so vital.

Some Days

I feel okay some days.
I don't feel engulfed by the loss or the shame.
It is as if I have been born anew.
Some days,
I find a reason to live,
And to not take my life.
Some days,
I find that my eyes have been opened just
enough that I can see the beauty.
The beauty in myself and in others.
I think to myself,
Maybe I can keep on living for the rest of my
life.

www.ingramcontent.com/pod-product-compliance
Lightning Source LLC
Chambersburg PA
CBHW051722130826
49812CB00034B/1306
* 9 7 8 9 3 5 7 2 1 3 2 5 7 *